BASIC GUIDE TO IRISH RECORDS
FOR
FAMILY HISTORY

by
Brian Mitchell

CLEARFIELD

Printed for
Clearfield Company by
Genealogical Publishing Co.
Baltimore, Maryland
2008

ISBN-13: 978-0-8063-5373-9
ISBN-10: 0-8063-5373-2

Made in the United States of America

Cover illustration: Tamlaght Finlagan Parish Church located in Ballykelly, County Londonderry; this site is the burial ground of the Hamiltons, the maternal ancestors of John Steinbeck. Photograph provided by Samuel Mitchell.

Table of Contents

List of Illustrations

Introduction

Three centuries of emigration from Ireland has resulted in a significant Irish Diaspora, numbering 70 million people, in countries such as the United States of America, Canada, Australia, New Zealand and Great Britain. Many descendants of these immigrants are keen to explore their Irish roots.

On 6 December 1921, with a treaty signed between Britain and Ireland, the partitioning of Ireland by the Government of Ireland Act of November 1920 came into effect. Two Home Rule parliaments were established: one for Northern Ireland that consisted of the counties of Antrim, Armagh, Down, Fermanagh, Londonderry (also referred to as Derry) and Tyrone; and the other for Southern Ireland, which consisted of the remaining twenty-six counties of Ireland. The powers of both parliaments were limited by Westminster.

In Southern Ireland reaction to the Anglo-Irish treaty effectively led to a civil war with the anti-treaty IRA (Irish Republican Army) seizing the Four Courts in Dublin in April 1922. This event, of course, was to have serious repercussions for family historians. Michael Collins ordered the pro-treaty Free State army to attack the Four Courts and drive the IRA out of Dublin. The shelling of the Four Courts on 28 June 1922, aided by two 18-pound guns lent by the British army, resulted in a fire and the destruction of many important historical documents, including many Church of Ireland registers, wills and early nineteenth-century census returns.

A primary aim of this book, however, is to dispel the widely-held notion that most records of genealogical interest in Ireland were destroyed; they weren't.

I also firmly believe that initiating research into your Irish ancestry is quite straightforward; in my opinion, there are eight major record sources to examine. These sources include the following items:

- Civil registers of births, marriages and deaths
- Church registers of baptisms, marriages and burials
- Gravestone inscriptions
- Wills
- 1901 and 1911 census returns
- Mid-nineteenth-century Griffith's Valuation
- Early nineteenth-century Tithe Applotment Books
- Other census substitutes

This book will examine each of these sources, which should be searched before you consider further research options.

These sources can all be examined in a total of five national repositories; three in Dublin—General Register Office, National Archives of Ireland and National Library of Ireland; and two in Belfast—General Register Office and Public Record Office of Northern Ireland. Prior to 1922 the records for all counties of Ireland were held in Dublin. The partitioning of Ireland and the creation of Northern Ireland resulted in the establishment of record offices in Belfast. This book will identify the major record collections held in each of these repositories.

This book also recognises the fact that family historians want to search databases online. In the ideal world there would be a single window electronic access to the record sources of Ireland along the lines of Scotland's www.scotlandspeople.gov.uk. There is not; but, as this book will show, there are a growing number of Irish record sources on the internet.

Getting Started

Irish family history research begins with building up a picture of the original immigrant in his or her adopted homeland.

Irish surnames can provide clues and insight into the origins of your family history. Surnames of Gaelic Irish origin frequently confirm membership of a sept, which Edward MacLysaght defined as "a group of persons who, or whose immediate and known ancestors, bore a common surname and inhabited the same locality." Thus, even today, Irish surnames are still very dominant and numerous in the very districts where their names originated.

By examining surname reference books or by using the "Surname search" facility on the Irish Times website at www.ireland.com/ancestor, you can build up a picture of the location and history of surnames in Ireland.

The key to unlocking Irish family history origins is the knowledge of place. In tracing your roots in Ireland, the most important piece of information to treasure, to be gleaned from either family folklore or record sources, is any information as to a place of origin of your ancestors.

Successful genealogical research is rooted in geography as all major Irish record sources are organised by what appears to be a confusing array of administrative divisions. Records of value to the family historian were gathered by one or more of these divisions (see Irish Administrative Divisions, pp. 37–38).

The author, for example, lives in the village of Eglinton, which is located in the townland of Muff (318 acres in size), in the civil parish of Faughanvale, in the Diocese of Derry, in the

Barony of Tirkeeran, in the district electoral division of Eglinton, in the registrar's district of Eglinton, in the poor law union of Londonderry, in the probate district of Londonderry, County Londonderry, Province of Ulster, Ireland.

From a family historian's perspective, the most effective way to view Ireland is as a country that is subdivided into counties, which in turn are subdivided into parishes, and which in turn are subdivided into townlands. The fact that many records of genealogical value were compiled on a parish basis means that realistic genealogical research, in the absence of indexing and databases, requires knowledge of the parish in which your ancestor lived. If sources are not indexed, you then need to know where your ancestor lived before you can begin to select appropriate records to search. As a general rule, the knowledge of the county of origin of your ancestor is insufficient information for locating records about them.

The *General Alphabetical Index To the Townlands and Towns, Parishes and Baronies of Ireland* (Alexander Thom, Dublin, 1861; reprinted by Genealogical Publishing Company, Baltimore, 1986) identifies all of Ireland's 60,462 townlands together with their first edition Ordnance Survey map number. The "Placenames" search facility listed on the internet at www.ireland.com/ancestor also allows you to search the entire Townland Index, together with street listings from Dublin, Cork and Belfast cities, more than 65,000 entries in all.

Between 1829 and 1842 Ordnance Survey Ireland completed the first ever large-scale (at 6 inches to 1 mile) survey of an entire country. These maps were surveyed on a county basis. You can purchase these first-edition, full-colour Irish Townland Maps at www.pasthomes.com. For example, to purchase the first edition map (dimensions 33" by 23") for the village of Eglinton, you select County Londonderry and OS sheet number 14.

The Ordnance Survey Ireland historic map archive at www.irishhistoricmaps.ie now contains the original pre-famine 6" mapping series (dated 1837–1842) and post-famine 25" survey (dated 1888–1913) for the Republic of Ireland (but not Northern Ireland). In addition to searching this resource by county and townland, you can also pan across the entire archive. To view the maps, you have to register and purchase credits (starting at €5 for 1 day up to €300 for 1 year). You can then print out selected sections or purchase hard copy maps for delivery by post.

Family historians are fascinated by passenger lists. Official passenger lists from Ireland only exist from 1890, and they are held in the Board of Trade records (reference BT27) in the National Archives, Kew, Surrey, England. These lists are arranged monthly by port of departure. Findmypast.com, in association with the National Archives, has now digitised and indexed these lists, which name 30 million long-haul passengers who left from 35 ports in the British Isles (which includes the Republic of Ireland until partition in 1921) between 1890 and 1960. The indexes to these passenger lists are searchable online, for free, at www.ancestorsonboard.com. These passenger lists (which record UK addresses from 1922) are searchable by name, port, ship and date.

As a general rule, prior to 1890, you are more likely to identify passengers at the port of arrival as opposed to the port of departure. By the mid-nineteenth century, 70% of Irish emigrants entered the U.S. through New York. The bulk of these passengers to New York are recorded on two websites; www.castlegarden.org

for arrivals prior to 1892 and www.ellisislandrecords.org for the time period 1892 to 1924.

The website of the Genealogical Publishing Company (www.genealogical.com) is also worth exploring as a keyword search for Passenger Lists returns 122 research results. This company has published numerous indexed volumes of passenger departures and immigrant arrivals. Furthermore, the "Name Search" facility on this website allows you to search, at no charge, the indexes to many of their books and CDs. For example, you can search their *Irish Immigrants to North America* index, which is composed of ten volumes of Irish passenger lists naming approximately 60,000 immigrants; the earliest list dates from 1735, the latest from 1871.

Advertisement for an Irish emigrant ship.

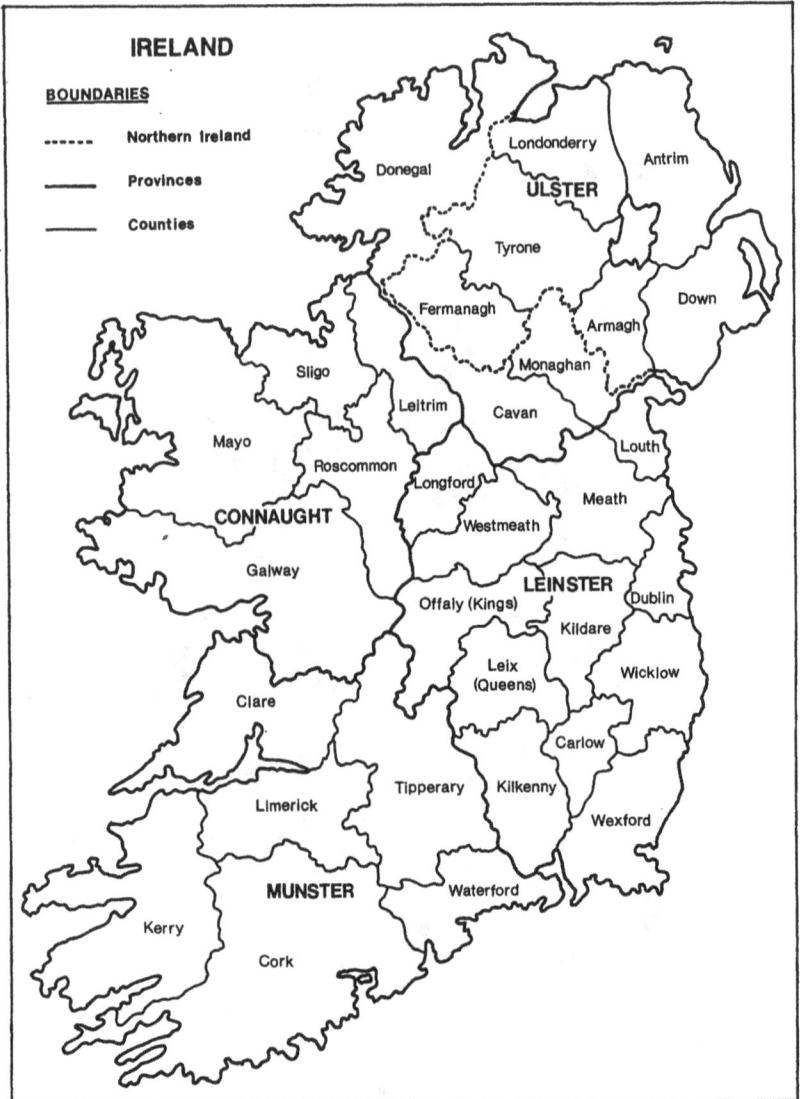

IRELAND

BOUNDARIES

- - - - - Northern Ireland

―――― Provinces

―――― Counties

Londonderry

Donegal

Antrim

ULSTER

Tyrone

Down

Fermanagh

Armagh

Monaghan

Sligo

Leitrim

Cavan

Louth

Mayo

Roscommon

Longford

Meath

CONNAUGHT

Westmeath

Galway

LEINSTER

Offaly (Kings)

Dublin

Kildare

Leix
(Queens)

Wicklow

Clare

Carlow

Tipperary

Kilkenny

Limerick

Wexford

MUNSTER

Waterford

Kerry

Cork

The Counties of Ireland

Family historians should view Ireland as a country
consisting of counties, parishes, and townlands.

CIVIL PARISHES

The Parishes of County Londonderry.

THE TOWNLANDS OF

1 Ardnaguniog
2 Ballygudden
3 Barnakilly
4 Bolie
5 Campsey Lower
6 Campsey Upper
7 Carmoney
8 Carnakilly Lower
9 Carnakilly Upper
10 Carnamuff
11 Carrickhugh
12 Clanterkee
13 Cloghole
14 Coolafinny

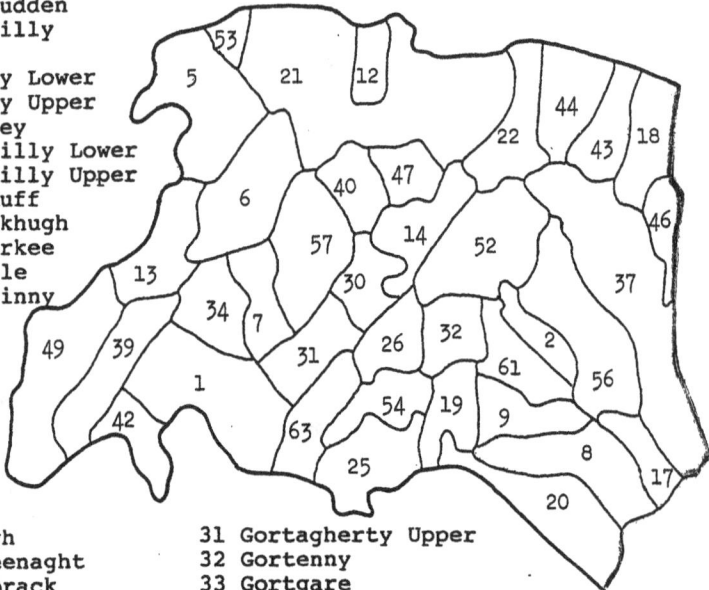

15 Coolagh
16 Coolkeenaght
17 Craigbrack
18 Cregan
19 Derryarkin Lower
20 Derryarkin Upper
21 Donnybrewer
22 Drummaneny
23 Dungullion
24 Dunlade Glebe
25 Falloward
26 Fallowlea
27 Faughanvale
28 Glasakeeran
29 Glebe
30 Gortagherty Lower

31 Gortagherty Upper
32 Gortenny
33 Gortgare
34 Greenan
35 Gresteel Beg
36 Gresteel More
37 Killylane
38 Killywool
39 Kilnappy
40 Laraghaleas
41 Legavannon
42 Ligg
43 Longfield Beg
44 Longfield More
45 Loughermore
46 Magheramore

The Townlands of Faughanvale Parish, County Londonderry.

FAUGHANVALE PARISH

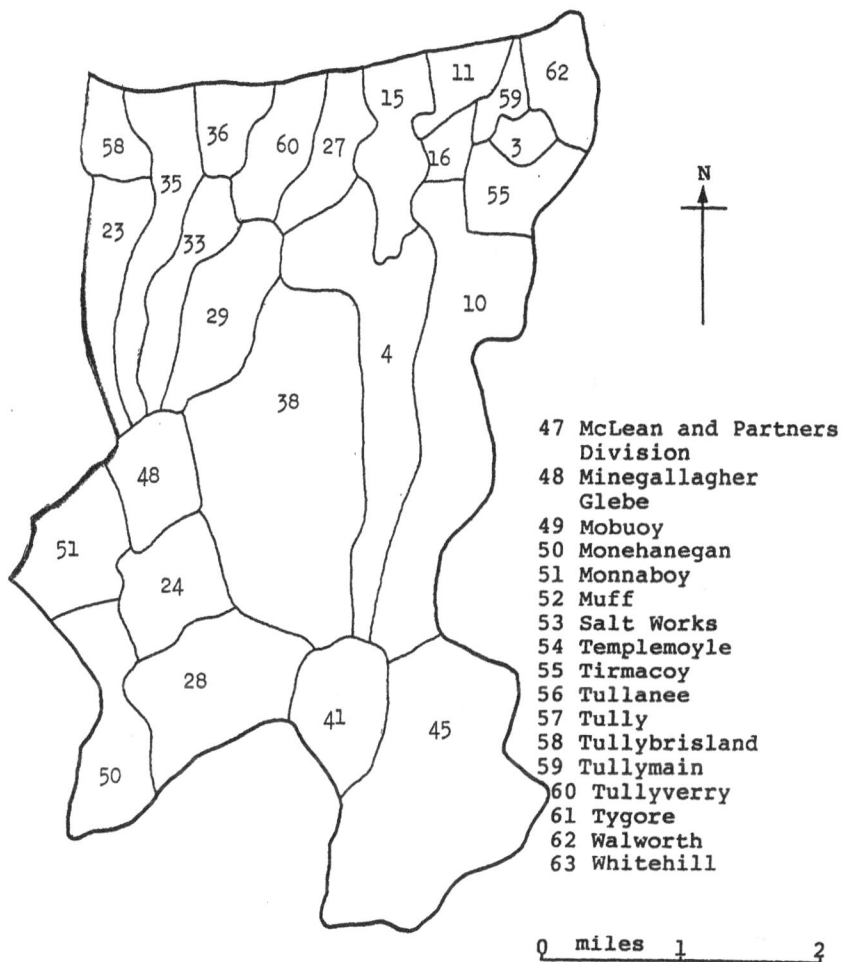

47 McLean and Partners
   Division
48 Minegallagher
   Glebe
49 Mobuoy
50 Monehanegan
51 Monnaboy
52 Muff
53 Salt Works
54 Templemoyle
55 Tirmacoy
56 Tullanee
57 Tully
58 Tullybrisland
59 Tullymain
60 Tullyverry
61 Tygore
62 Walworth
63 Whitehill

0   miles   1   2

The Main Sources

In this section I will detail the major Irish record sources in terms of what information they contain, their limitations, where they can be found and how they can be accessed.

Civil Registers of Births, Marriages and Deaths

Civil registration in Ireland of births, deaths and Roman Catholic marriages began on 1 January 1864, while Protestant marriages were subject to registration from 1 April 1845. For the purpose of civil registration, Ireland was divided into about 800 registrar districts, which were grouped into 140 poor law unions.

The details included in birth, marriage and death certificates, together with their associated indexes, help to make this source an ideal starting point in researching Irish ancestors.

A birth certificate provides the name, date of birth and place of birth of the child together with the father's name, occupation and residence and the mother's name and maiden name.

A marriage certificate gives the date and place of marriage and the names, ages, occupations and residences of the bride and groom together with the names and occupations of their fathers and the names of two witnesses.

A death certificate supplies the deceased's name, age, occupation, date of death, place of death and cause of death.

The certificates, therefore, vary in the amount and usefulness of information provided. Death certificates offer the minimum of information and, in many cases, are only useful as a means to get an approximate date of birth of an ancestor from the age given at death.

Civil birth, marriage and death certificates are indexed; the early indexes were compiled annually, while the later ones (from 1878) were arranged by quarter year. They are arranged in alphabetical order by surname and then by Christian name.

In the time period 1864 to 1902 and 1928 to 1966, the indexes to births, marriages and deaths list the year (quarter year from 1878) of registration of the event; the name; the poor law union in which the event was registered; and the volume and page number in which the event will be found. The indexes for 1903 to 1927 provide additional information such as the date of the event; mother's maiden name in birth indexes; partner's surname in marriage indexes; and age and marital condition of deceased in death indexes.

It is clear that the indexes, especially prior to 1902, give limited information. A birth or death, for example, will be hard to identify without a fairly clear idea of when and where it happened. Furthermore the only guidance to an address in the indexes is the poor law union in which the event was registered. This means, for example, that the only address information provided in the indexes to events in County Wicklow are the five poor law union names of Baltinglass, Naas, Rathdown, Rathdrum and Shillelagh.

On the other hand, as the marriage indexes will list both parties (in their appropriate alphabetical placing), there is a cross-referencing system that may enable the identification of a marriage in the absence of both an address and date.

The General Register Offices in both Belfast and Dublin are committed to providing access to their records over the internet, but as yet there is no time scale for doing so.

Thus, at present, the indexes to civil registers for both Northern Ireland and the Republic of Ireland can not be accessed on the internet. The indexes can be searched in the Belfast and Dublin offices of the General Register Office on payment of the appropriate search fees (see Major Record Offices, pp. 39–42).

The International Genealogical Index (which can be searched online at www.familysearch.org), compiled by the Church of Jesus Christ of Latter-Days Saints (Mormons), includes some Irish civil registration records: births from 1864 to 1874 and marriages 1845 to 1850, 1855, 1863 and 1864.

Many of Ireland's network of county-based genealogy centres are computerising pre-1922 civil registers for their localities. Contact details for these centres can be found at www.irish-roots.net.

Church Registers of Baptisms, Marriages and Burials

Before the introduction of civil registration, many churches maintained registers of baptisms, marriages, and sometimes burials.

A baptism entry can provide the name of the child; date of baptism; date of birth; parents' names, including maiden name of mother; parents' address (by townland); occupation; and names of sponsors (particularly in Roman Catholic registers).

A marriage entry can provide the names of the bride and groom, their places of residence, date of marriage, parents' names, and names of witnesses.

A burial entry can provide the name and residence of the deceased, burial date and place, and age of the deceased. In the case of children, the names of parents may be included.

Church registers, like civil registers, clearly supply enough information to build and confirm family linkages.

It must be emphasised that dates of commencement and quality of information in church registers vary from parish to parish and from denomination to denomination. This source, however, should always be checked if you know the civil parish address and religious denomination of your ancestor. *A Guide to Irish Parish Registers* (Brian Mitchell, Genealogical Publishing Company, Baltimore, 1988; reprinted 2001) attempts, on a county basis, to locate churches of all denominations within their civil parishes and to provide the earliest commencement date of their registers.

Church of Ireland registers prior to 1 January 1871 are public records. It is true that 1,002 pre-1870 Church of Ireland registers were destroyed in Dublin in 1922. However, despite the fire, many registers of great age have survived.

Church of Ireland parishes normally conform to the civil parish, though Roman Catholic parishes do not, as they are generally larger. The Roman Catholic Church, owing to the Reformation of the sixteenth century, had to adapt itself to a new structure centred on towns and villages. The Presbyterian church doesn't have a parish structure, with the congregations generally forming where there was sufficient demand from local Presbyterian families. Thus it is very noticeable that the Presbyterian congregations in Ireland are very much associated with the nine counties of the northern province of Ulster.

The National Library of Ireland holds microfilm copy of the registers of most Roman Catholic parishes in Ireland for years up to 1880. The National Archives of Ireland holds originals, microfilm copy, transcripts and abstracts of many Church of Ireland registers. The Public Record Office of Northern Ireland holds microfilm copies of the majority of church registers of all denominations for the nine counties of Ulster.

There is no national index to church registers. To date, only the county-based genealogy centres have attempted any large scale, systematic indexing of church registers in their localities. The Irish Family History Foundation is now planning to offer, on a phased basis, pay-per-view searches of the databases created by the county genealogy centres on their website www.irish-roots.net.

Indexes to the church registers (containing over 3 million records) computerised by the local genealogy centres for counties Armagh, Cavan, Derry, Fermanagh, Leitrim, Limerick, Mayo, Sligo, Tyrone and Wexford can be searched for free at www.irishgenealogy.ie.

As part of its record extraction programme, the Mormons have computerised some Irish parish registers. In the International Genealogical Index (www.familysearch.org), clicking on "Source Call Number" in the "Source Information" section against any selected individual will enable researchers to tell if the information was extracted from a church register or from a civil register or from information submitted by an individual.

Birth Certificate of Robert Graham Moore of Calhame.

The Townland of Calhame (spelt as Caulhame on maps today) is located in the civil parish of Desertoghill, County Londonderry, and is situated two miles east of the town of Garvagh. Robert Graham Moore was my wife's grandfather.

*Marriage Certificate of Joseph Moore
and Elizabeth Graham of Calhame.*

Gravestone Inscriptions

With civil registration of births and deaths commencing in 1864 and with the patchy survival of church records prior to 1820, gravestone inscriptions take on a special significance. Many Church of Ireland burial registers were destroyed in 1922, while the registers of the Roman Catholic and Presbyterian churches are especially poor regarding burial entries.

In many cases a gravestone inscription will be the only record of an ancestor's death. Yet gravestones offer much more than just the date of death; they frequently mention the townland address of the deceased together with the names, ages, and dates of death of other family members. Many graves are family plots, and as a consequence list family members and their relationship to each other.

Church of Ireland graveyards should be examined irrespective of an ancestor's religion. Prior to the 1820s, owing to the operation of the Penal Laws, both Catholics and Presbyterians shared the same graveyards. Prior to the Burial Act of 1868, which permitted dissenting (i.e., Presbyterian) ministers to conduct burial services, the Church of Ireland clergy held jurisdiction over funeral services for all Protestants. It is, unfortunately, true that the unkempt state of many graveyards (especially those now isolated from a functioning church) and the weathering of headstones precludes the reading of many inscriptions. It must also be said that only a small percentage of burials in any graveyard are marked by headstones.

After identifying an ancestor's residence (i.e., townland or parish), researchers should visit the local graveyards.

The *Journal of the Association for the Preservation of the Memorials of the Dead*, during over forty-seven years of its existence between 1888 and 1934, published more than 10,000 gravestone inscriptions collected from all over Ireland. A composite index to surnames and places for the first twenty years of publication was published in 1910. The National Library of Ireland holds a complete set of this journal.

The largest collections of indexed transcripts of gravestone inscriptions in Ireland are held by the county genealogy centres. Irish World of Coalisland, County Tyrone and the Ulster Historical Foundation of Belfast have transcribed the largest volume of gravestone inscriptions; they can be searched online at www.irishgenealogy.ie and www.historyfromheadstones.com, respectively. In both cases, searching of the indexes is free, but researchers have to buy full inscription details. As both organisations have transcribed the inscriptions of over 800 graveyards from the six counties of Northern Ireland, there will be a high degree of overlap.

Wills

Wills, by listing relatives—brothers, sisters, children and even grandchildren—are very valuable documents. It must be said that only a small proportion of the population—usually the better-off, such as gentry, farmers and merchants—made wills. Although there is no guarantee that your ancestor made a will, I would recommend a search of the indexes that exist.

Before 1857, ecclesiastical courts of the Church of Ireland, based in each diocese, were in charge of all testamentary affairs. Although most of these wills were destroyed in 1922, the indexes to these wills were not destroyed, and they are available in the

National Archives of Ireland. The Irish Wills Index to testamentary records in the National Archives of Ireland for the time period 1484 to 1858 contains over 102,000 names and can be searched, by subscription, on the Irish Origins website at www.irishorigins.com.

The "Name Search" facility at www.genealogical.com allows you to search, for free, the index to *Irish Source Records* which includes Indexes to Irish Wills, 1536–1857, and Index to the Prerogative Wills of Ireland, 1536–1810.

In 1858 testamentary jurisdiction was transferred to a principal registry in Dublin and eleven district registries. From that date yearly calendars of wills and administrations were published in printed volumes in alphabetical order by surname and Christian name. These indexes provide the name, address, occupation and date of death of the deceased.

A complete set of these calendars for the whole of Ireland up to 1917 are held in both the National Archives of Ireland as well as the Public Record Office of Northern Ireland. The indexes from 1918 for the twenty-six counties of the Republic of Ireland and for the six counties of Northern Ireland are held in the National Archives of Ireland and the Public Record Office of Northern Ireland, respectively. These calendars can be a useful means to identify, relatively quickly, the date of death of an ancestor.

Wills and/or copies of will books survive for all districts, except for those wills proved in the Dublin registry prior to 1922. The Public Record Office of Northern Ireland holds the will books for the districts of Armagh, Belfast and Londonderry, and the National Archives of Ireland has the will books for the remaining eight district registries in the Republic of Ireland.

1901 and 1911 Census Returns

Although census enumerations were carried out every decade from 1821, the earliest surviving complete return for all Ireland is that of 1901. These returns were arranged by townland in rural areas and by street in urban areas.

The 1901 census records for each member of the household the name, age, religion, education, occupation, marital status and county or city of birth. The 1911 census provides additional information on the marriage; namely, the number of years married, the number of children born and the number still living.

The 1901 and 1911 census returns should be examined once you have established where your ancestor lived at the turn of the twentieth century.

The National Archives of Ireland holds the manuscript returns of the 1901 and 1911 censuses for all counties. The Public Record Office of Northern Ireland holds copies of the 1901 census returns for the six counties of Northern Ireland. The 1911 census returns for Northern Ireland can only be viewed in the National Archives in Dublin.

The National Archives of Ireland, in association with Library and Archives Canada, is currently digitising and indexing the 1901 and 1911 census records of Ireland. Every name, age and place information will be indexed, and 4,500 reels of microfilm containing six million images will be digitised. Starting in Autumn 2007 with the 1911 census returns for Dublin City and County, the 1901 and 1911 census returns for all counties of Ireland will be made available, at no charge, on the internet over the next three years (check www.nationalarchives.ie for updates).

	NAME and SURNAME	RELATION to Head of Family	RELIGIOUS PROFESSION.	EDUCATION.	AGE.
1	Joseph Moore	Head of Family	Presbyterian	Read & Write	57
2	Elizabeth Moore	Wife	Presbyterian	Read & Write	51
3	Fanny Moore	Daughter	Presbyterian	read & Write	22
4	Robert Moore	Son	Presbyterian	Read & Write	18
5	Anna M. Moore	Daughter	Presbyterian	Read & Write	6
6					
7					
8					
9					
10					
11					
12					
13					
14					
15					

I hereby certify, as required by the Act 63 Vic., cap. 6, a. 6 (1), that the foregoing Return is correct, according to the best of my knowledge and belief.

John Hutchinson Const (Signature of Enumerator.)

The 1901 Census Return for the Moore family of Calhame.

IRELAND, 1901.

(filling up this Table are given on the other side.)

FORM A.

No. on Form B. *1*

who slept or abode in this House on the night of SUNDAY, the 31st of MARCH 1901

SEX.	RANK, PROFESSION, OR OCCUPATION.	MARRIAGE	WHERE BORN.	IRISH LANGUAGE.	If Deaf and Dumb; Dumb only; Blind; Imbecile or Idiot; or Lunatic.
Write "M" for Males and "F" for Females.	State the Particular Rank, Profession, Trade, or other Employment of each person. Children or young person attending a School, or receiving regular instruction at home, should be returned as Scholars. Before filling this column you are requested to read the instructions on the other side.	Whether "Married," "Widower," "Widow," or "Not Married."	If in Ireland, state in what County or City; if elsewhere, state the name of the Country.	Write the word "IRISH" in this column opposite the name of each person who speaks IRISH only, and the words "IRISH & ENGLISH" opposite the names of those who can speak both languages. In other cases no entry should be made in this column.	Write the respective infirmities opposite the name of the afflicted person.
M	Farmer	Married	Co Derry		
F		Married	Co Derry		
F	Dressmaker	Not Married	Co Derry		
M	Farm Labourer	Not Married	Co Derry		
F	Scholar	Not Married	Co Derry		

I believe the foregoing to be a true Return.

Joseph Moore (Signature of Head of Family).

	NAME AND SURNAME.		RELATION to Head of Family.	RELIGIOUS PROFESSION.	EDUCATION.	AGE (last Birthday) and SEX.	
	No Persons ABSENT on the Night of Sunday, April 2nd, to be entered here; EXCEPT those (not enumerated elsewhere) who may be out at WORK or TRAVELLING, &c., during that Night, and who RETURN HOME on MONDAY, APRIL 3RD. *Subject to the above instruction, the Name of the Head of the Family should be written first; then the names of his Wife, Children, and other Relatives; then those of Visitors, Boarders, Servants, &c.*		State whether "Head of Family," or "Wife," or "Son," "Daughter," or other Relative; "Visitor," "Boarder," "Servant," &c.	State here the particular Religion, or Religious Denomination, to which each person belongs. [Members of Protestant Denominations are requested not to describe themselves by the vague term "Protestant," but to enter the name of the Particular Church, Denomination, or Body to which they belong.]	State here whether he or she can "Read and Write," can "Read" only, or "Cannot Read."	Insert Age opposite each name—the Ages of Males in column 6, and the Ages of Females in column 7. For Infants under one year state the age in months, as "under 1 month," "1 month," "2 months," &c.	
						Ages of Males.	Ages of Females.
	Christian Name.	Surname.					
	1.	2.	3.	4.	5.	6.	7.
1	▉▉▉▉▉	▉▉▉▉	Head of family	Presbyterian	Read & write	64	
2	Elizabeth	Moore	Wife	Presbyterian	Read & write		61
3	Robert C	Moore	Son	Presbyterian	Read & write	28	
4	Anna M	Moore	Daughter	Presbyterian	Read & write	—	16
5							
6							
7							
8							
9							
10							
11							
12							
13							
14							
15							

I hereby certify, as required by the Act 19 Edw. VII., and 1 Geo. V., cap. 11, that the foregoing Return is correct, according to the best of my knowledge and belief.

Daniel Kelly Const.   Signature   Enumerator.

The 1911 Census Return for the Moore family of Calhame.

IRELAND, 1911.

filling up this Table are given on the other side.

FORM A.

&c., who slept or abode in this House on the night of SUNDAY, the 2nd of APRIL, 1911.

No. on Form B. _11_

RANK, PROFESSION, OR OCCUPATION.	PARTICULARS AS TO MARRIAGE.				WHERE BORN.	IRISH LANGUAGE.	If Deaf and Dumb; Dumb only; Blind; Imbecile or Idiot; or Lunatic.
State the particular Rank, Profession, Trade, or other Employment of each person. Children or young persons attending a School, or receiving regular instruction at home, should be returned as Scholars. [No entry should be made in the case of wives, daughters, or other female relatives solely engaged in domestic duties at home.] Before filling this column you are requested to read the instructions on the other side.	Whether "Married," "Widower," "Widow," or "Single."	Completed years the present Marriage has lasted. If less than one year, write "under one."	Children born alive to present Marriage. If no children born alive, write "None" in column 11.		If in Ireland, state in what County or City; if elsewhere, state the name of the Country.	Write the word "Irish" in this column opposite the name of each person who speaks Irish only, and the words "Irish & English" opposite the names of those who can speak both languages. In other cases no entry should be made in this column.	Write the respective infirmities opposite the name of the afflicted person.
			Total Children born alive.	Children still living.			
9.	10.	11.	12.	13.	14.	15.
Farmer	Married	—	—	—	Co Derry	—	✓
	Married	27	5	3	Co Derry		
Farmer	Single				Co Derry	●	—
	Single				Co Derry	—	

I believe the foregoing to be a true Return.

Josiah Moore Signature of Head of Family.

Mid-Nineteenth-Century Griffith's Valuation

The first four censuses of Ireland (i.e., censuses for the years 1821, 1831, 1841 and 1851) were largely destroyed in the fire in 1922; and those censuses for years 1861, 1871, 1881 and 1891 were destroyed by order of the government. Owing to this loss, Griffith's Valuation has become a record of extreme importance to family researchers. It is, in effect, a census substitute for post-Famine Ireland.

Griffith's Primary Valuation of Ireland was a survey carried out, for the purpose of calculating rates, in every parish in Ireland between 1848 and 1864; it detailed every head of household and occupier of land, against their townland address in rural areas and against their street address in urban areas. The results of the survey were published in volumes by poor law union.

This source lists the names of heads of household only; it doesn't name any other members in a household. This source is widely available in the major libraries and record offices throughout Ireland.

Maps were compiled to accompany Griffith's Valuation; this procedure means that the locations of all properties in the mid-nineteenth century—houses and farms—can be identified once you have found your ancestor in the survey.

Irish Origins at www.irishorigins.com provides access, by subscription, to the Griffith's Primary Valuation of Ireland and the maps associated with the survey. Subscription packages range from £7.50 for 72 hours to £34.50 for 1 year.

The "Name Search" facility at www.genealogical.com allows you to search, for free, the index to *Griffith's Valuation of Ireland, 1848–1864*. This index contains over 1.25 million names for the thirty-two counties of Ireland.

VALUATION OF TENEMENTS.

PARISH OF BANAGHER.

No. and Letters of Reference to Map.	Names — Townlands and Occupiers.	Names — Immediate Lessors.	Description of Tenement.	Area — A. R. P.	Rateable Annual Valuation — Land. £ s. d.	Rateable Annual Valuation — Buildings. £ s. d.	Total Annual Valuation of Rateable Property. £ s. d.
	COOLNAMONAN—*continued.*						
8 A	Jas. Hassan (*Tonry Due*),	Trustees Robt. Ogilby,	House, offices, & land,	2 1 10	1 7 0	—	
— B				2 1 20	0 16 0	—	
— C				9 0 20	3 10 0	—	
— D				5 1 20	1 2 0	—	} 7 15 0
8 a / 18 f				0 0 30	0 2 0	0 18 0	
9 A	John Hassan,	James Hassan,	House,		0 5 0	0 5 0	0 5 0
— B	Patrick Hassan,	Trustees Robt. Ogilby,	House, offices, & land,	5 3 30	4 0 0	—	
— C				4 1 30	2 1 0	—	
— D				4 1 0	1 16 0	—	
— E				9 0 30	3 10 0	—	
— F				5 3 35	1 1 0	—	} 13 10 0
— G				7 0 15	0 5 0	0 8 0	
18 d				5 0 35	0 8 0		
10 A	Thomas Hassan,	Same,	House, offices, & land,	1 0 30	0 2 0	—	
— B				1 1 20	0 17 0	—	
— C				5 3 30	0 18 0	—	} 4 10 0
— D				3 3 25	2 0 0	0 8 0	
18 e				0 0 25	0 4 0		
11 A	James M'Clusky,	Same,	House, offices, & land,	4 1 10	0 2 0	—	
— B				3 2 10	2 16 0	—	} 7 15 0
— C				14 1 10	0 10 0	0 10 0	
13 h / o a	Hugh M'Clusky,	James M'Clusky,	House,	0 2 25	0 2 0	0 5 0	0 5 0
12 A	Michl. Hassan (*Jack Roe*),	Trustees Robt. Ogilby,	House, office, & land,	1 0 15	0 15 0	—	} 2 5 0
— B / 18 c				2 3 20	1 5 0	0 5 0	
13 g	Nelus Hasson,	Free,	Waste of hos., streets, &c.	1 3 10	—	—	} 0 10 0
—			House and garden,	0 0 35	0 5 0	0 5 0	

Griffith's Valuation, published in 1858, for the townland of Coolnamonan.

No.	Tenant	Immediate Lessor	Description of Tenement									
14	Alick Hassan,	Trustees Robt. Ogilby,	Land,									
15 A/B	John Hassan,	Same,	House, offices, & land,									
16	Michael Hassan (*Roe*),	Same,	House, offices, & land,									
17 A	James Hassan (*Tailor*),	Michael Hassan (*Roe*),	House, offices, & land,									
18 A/B	Hugh M'Clusky,	Same,	House, offices, & land,									
19	Charles Donnelly,	Trustees Robt. Ogilby,	Land,									
20 A	Owen Sharkey,	Same,	House, offices, & land,									
– B	Denis M'Clusky,	Same,	House, offices, and land,									
21/22	Michael Donohoe,	Same,	Land,									
			Total,							373	3 33	123	5

TAMNYAGAN.
(*Ord. S. 80.*)

No.	Tenant	Immediate Lessor	Description of Tenement
1	Thomas Creighton,	Trustees Robt. Ogilby,	House, offices, and land,
2	Joseph Hill,	Same,	House, offices, & land,
3	Joseph Dunn,	Same,	House, offices, and land,
4	John Kane (*Patt*),	Same,	House, offices, and land,
5	Patrick Kane,	Same,	House, offices, and land,
6	Mary Mullen,	Same,	House, offices, and land,
7	Patrick Mullen,	Same,	House, offices, and land,
8	Patrick Kane, / John Kane (*Patt*), / Mary Mullen,	Same,	Mountain,
9	Patrick Kane, / Arthur Kane,	Same	House, offices, and land,
10	Anne Kane,	Same,	House, office, & garden, / Land,
11	John Kane (*Quinton*), / Arthur Kane,	Same,	House, offices, and land,
12	Michael Kane, / John Kane (*Quinton*),	Same,	Mountain,

The townland of Coolnamonan is located in the civil parish of Banagher, County Londonderry, and is situated five miles southwest of the town of Dungiven. Nine Hassan households were farming in Coolnamonan in 1858.

HASSAN FARMS IN COOLNAMONAN
1858

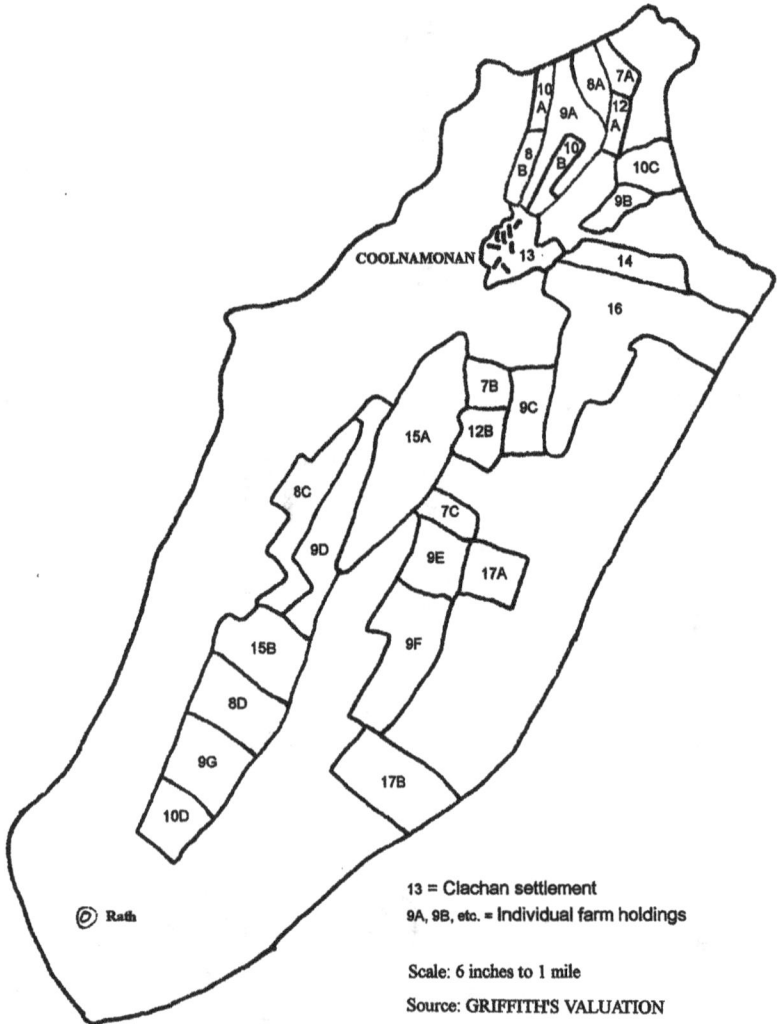

Griffith's Valuation Map of Hassan farms in Coolnamonan in 1858.

In 1858, eight Hassan households were living in the village of Coolnamonan (number 13 on map). Although dispersed farms dominate the Irish landscape today, such clusters of farmhouses in "farm towns," called clachans, were historically the dominant form of rural settlement in Ireland.

Early Nineteenth-Century Tithe Applotment Books

Owing to the destruction of most early nineteenth-century census returns, the Tithe Books are now seen by researchers as a census substitute for pre-Famine rural Ireland.

The Tithe Applotment Books were compiled between 1823 and 1837 by civil parish, and they list all landholders, against their townland address, who paid tithe. Tithe was a tax, based on land valuation and paid by all, irrespective of religious denomination, for the support of the Established Church (i.e., Church of Ireland).

The Tithe Books will record the names of tenant farmers but not of urban dwellers or landless labourers. Some landholders may also appear more than once on a list, thereby indicating that they held more than one piece of land. The results of this assessment were published in volumes by parish.

This source lists the names of heads of household only; it doesn't name any other members in a household. Copies of the Tithe Books are available in the National Archives of Ireland and the National Library of Ireland; Tithe Books for the nine counties of Ulster are held in the Public Record Office of Northern Ireland.

The "Name Search" facility at www.genealogical.com allows you to search, for free, the index to *Tithe Applotment Books, 1823–1838*. This index contains 200,000 entries extracted from Tithe Books of 233 parishes in the six counties of Northern Ireland.

Other Census Substitutes

Any surviving fragments from the censuses of 1821 to 1851 are held in the National Archives of Ireland with microfilm copies in the Public Record Office of Northern Ireland.

Pension search summaries act as a partial reconstruction of the 1841 and 1851 censuses. The Old Age Pension Act was introduced in 1908. For persons applying to the local Pensions Officer for a pension with no proof of age (i.e., that they were over seventy years old), searches were requested of the 1841 and 1851 censuses at the Public Record Office, Dublin. These searches were all completed before the fire in 1922.

The Old Age Pension search summaries for the Republic of Ireland are held in the National Archives of Ireland; those for Northern Ireland are held in the Public Record Office of Northern Ireland.

An index to these Old Age Pension search summaries (1841/1851 Census Abstracts) for both Northern Ireland and the Republic of Ireland are available online. The "Name Search" facility at www.genealogical.com allows you to search, for free, the index to *Irish Source Records* which includes 1841/1851 Census Abstracts for both Northern Ireland and the Republic of Ireland.

As many parishes have no church registers predating 1800, it is quite possible that you will not be able to link with any degree of certainty your family connections back through the seventeenth and eighteenth centuries in Ireland.

There are, however, a number of census records and census substitutes, usually compiled by civil parish, which can be searched for the eighteenth century and earlier. Note the following examples.

- Flax Growers Lists of 1796: This source lists farmers who were entitled to a grant, in the form of equipment, for the sowing of flax seed. The "Name Search" facility at www.genealogical.com allows you to search, for free, the index to *Irish Flax Growers Lists, 1796*. This index names 60,000 individuals from all counties in Ireland except Dublin and Wicklow.
- Religious Census of 1766: Compiled by Church of Ireland rectors, these returns list heads of household and their religion.
- Protestant Householders Lists of 1740.
- Hearth Money Rolls of the 1660s: Lists those households liable to a tax of two shillings, which was raised for every hearth or fireplace.
- Muster Rolls of 1630: Lists the principal landlords in Ulster and the names of the men they could assemble in an emergency.

The one significant weakness of all census substitutes is that they list the names of heads of household only. As no information is provided on family members within each household or relationships between householders, it is not possible to confirm the nature of linkages between named people in these sources. Census substitutes, however, will be very useful in confirming the presence of a family name in a particular area and in providing some insight into the frequency and distribution of surnames.

You will find any surviving copies of these sources in the National Archives of Ireland, the National Library of Ireland and the Public Record Office of Northern Ireland.

To sum up, there are two essential aspects to Irish family history research: (1) the search for birth, marriage and death events and (2) an examination of census returns and census substitutes for the locality (i.e., townland and parish) in which your ancestor resided.

Irish Administrative Divisions

These areas form the geographical basis for research. Records of value to the family historian were gathered by one or more of these seven divisions.

PROVINCE   The largest geographical division. Ireland is divided into four provinces: Connacht, Leinster, Munster and Ulster.

COUNTY   Ireland is divided into thirty-two counties. This division, begun in the twelfth century, reflected the imposition of the English system of local government in Ireland. The county boundaries reflected the lordships of the major Gaelic families.

BARONY   This subdivision of a county is now an obsolete division, but in the nineteenth century it was widely used. Ireland was divided into 327 baronies that tended to reflect the holdings of the Irish clans. Both baronies and counties became established in the government land surveys of the seventeenth century.

PARISH   The knowledge of the parish address of their ancestor allows researchers to select record sources to examine. Ireland was divided into 2,428 civil parishes. Most record sources, both civil and church, of value to family historians were compiled and recorded by parish. (Ecclesiastical parishes were grouped into dioceses.)

TOWNLAND   The smallest and most ancient land
                             division in Ireland. Parishes were, in
                             effect, subdivided into townlands, a
                             few hundred acres in extent. There are
                             60,462 townlands in Ireland. By
                             identifying a townland address,
                             researchers have effectively identified
                             the ancestral home.

POOR LAW UNION   Districts, centred on a large market
                             town, were created in 1838 for the
                             financial support of the poor. Ireland
                             was originally divided into 130 Poor
                             Law Unions. In 1898 the poor law
                             union replaced the civil parish and
                             barony as the basic unit of local
                             government. Poor law unions were
                             subdivided into 829 Registration
                             Districts (to gather civil birth,
                             marriage and death details) and 3,751
                             District Electoral Divisions (to gather
                             census returns).

PROBATE DISTRICT   Created in 1858 for the purpose of
                             proving wills. There were twelve
                             probate districts in Ireland.

The Major Record Offices

General Register Office
Joyce House, 8–11 Lombard Street East, Dublin 2, Ireland.
Telephone: 00 353 1635 4423
Website: www.groireland.ie
Email: gro@health.irlgov.ie

Research Room: Open Monday to Friday 9.30 am to 4.30 pm.
(Note: Head office and postal enquiries to General Register
Office, Government Offices, Convent Road, Roscommon,
Tel: 00 353 90663 2900).

Sources:
Births and deaths registered in whole of Ireland from 1
January 1864 to 31 December 1921. Marriages registered in
whole of Ireland from 1 April 1845 to 31 December 1921.
Births, marriages and deaths for Ireland (excluding Northern
Ireland) from 1 January 1922.

Fees:
A particular search of indexes for 5 years €2.00.
A general search of indexes for 1 day covering all years €20.00.
A photocopy of an identified entry €6.00.

General Register Office
Oxford House, 49-55 Chichester Street, Belfast, BT1 4HL,
Northern Ireland.
Telephone: 028 9025 2000
Website: www.groni.gov.uk
Email: gro.nisra@dfpni.gov.uk

Research Room: Open Monday to Friday 9.30 am to 4.00 pm
(The indexes are computerised. As there are limited spaces
in the search room, it is advisable to book, telephone 028
9025 2128).

Sources:
Birth and death registers for the six counties of Northern Ireland from 1 January 1864 to the present day and civil marriage registers for Northern Ireland from 1st January 1922 to the present day. Marriages registered from 1 April 1845 to 31 December 1921 are held in the District Registrars' Offices.

Fees:
Computerised indexes can be searched for six hours at cost of £10.00. This cost includes four verifications of entries by staff with the option of further verifications at £2.50 each.

Assisted search of records with member of staff at £24 per hour.

National Archives of Ireland
Bishop Street, Dublin 8, Ireland
Telephone: 00 353 1407 2300
Website: www.nationalarchives.ie
Email: mail@nationalarchives.ie

Opening Hours: Monday to Friday 10.00 am to 5.00 pm.

Sources:
This office's collection is very extensive and of all-Ireland significance. It holds wills, Church of Ireland registers, 1901 and 1911 census returns, Griffith's Valuation, Tithe Books, and surviving nineteenth century census returns.

The National Archives provides a Genealogy Service where members of the public can consult a professional genealogist about sources relating to their family history. It is free and open to the public Monday to Friday from 10.00 am to 5.00 pm.

National Library of Ireland
Kildare Street, Dublin 2, Ireland
Telephone: 00 353 1603 0200
Website: www.nli.ie
Email: info@nli.ie

Opening Hours: Monday to Wednesday 10.00 am to 9.00 pm.
Thursday to Friday 10.00 am to 5.00 pm.
Saturday 10.00 am to 1.00 pm.

Sources:
Microfilm copy of the registers of most Roman Catholic parishes in Ireland for years up to 1880. In case of Diocese of Kerry and Diocese of Cloyne, researchers need permission of the Bishop to view relevant parish registers. In case of Archdiocese of Cashel and Emly, researchers must contact Tipperary Family History Research (All contact details are given on the National Library's website). The library also has copies of Griffith's Valuation and Tithe Books. In addition, it holds a comprehensive collection of directories, photographs, newspapers, maps and manuscripts.

The National Library provides a Genealogy Service where members of the public can consult a professional genealogist about sources relating to their family history. It is free and open to the public Monday to Friday from 10.00 am to 4.45 pm and Saturday 10.00 am to 12.30 pm.

Public Record Office of Northern Ireland
66 Balmoral Avenue, Belfast, BT9 6NY, Northern Ireland.
Telephone: 028 9025 1318
Website: www.proni.gov.uk
Email: proni@dcalni.gov.uk

Opening Hours: Monday, Tuesday, Wednesday and Friday 9.15 am to 4.45 pm; Thursday 10.00 am to 8.45 pm.

Sources:
This office's collection relates mainly to the nine counties of the province of Ulster (i.e., Counties Antrim, Armagh, Down, Fermanagh, Londonderry and Tyrone in Northern Ireland and Counties Cavan, Donegal and Monaghan in the Republic of Ireland). It holds wills, microfilm copies of most church registers of all religious denominations, microfilm copy of 1901 census returns (for Northern Ireland only), Griffith's Valuation, Griffith's Valuation maps (for Northern Ireland only), Tithe Books, and surviving nineteenth-century census returns.

An index of Church of Ireland and Presbyterian churches whose registers have been microfilmed by Public Record Office of Northern Ireland can be accessed on their website.

Irish Genealogy Centres

A network of county-based family history research centres have been established in Ireland. Details of their research services can be found online at www.irish-roots.net and www.irishgenealogy.ie.

County	Contact Details
Antrim	Ulster Historical Foundation, 7 Cotton Court, Belfast, BT1 2ED, Northern Ireland Tel: 028 9033 2288 Web: www.ancestryireland.com Email: enquiry@uhf.org.uk
Armagh	Armagh Ancestry, 40 English Street, Armagh, BT61 7BA, Northern Ireland Tel: 028 3752 1800 Web: www.visitarmagh.com Email: ancestry@armagh.gov.uk
Carlow	Carlow Genealogy Project. Currently closed.
Cavan	Cavan Genealogy, 1st Floor, Johnston Central Library, Farnham Street, Cavan, County Cavan Tel: 049 4361094 Email: cavangenealogy@eircom.net
Clare	Clare Heritage Centre, Church Street, Corofin, County Clare Tel: 065 6837955 Email: clareheritage@eircom.net
Cork City	Cork City Ancestral Project, c/o Cork County Library, Farranlea Road, Cork, County Cork Tel: 021 4346435 Email: corkancestry@ireland.com

Cork North	Mallow Heritage Centre, 27-28 Bank Place, Mallow, County Cork Tel: 022 50302 Email: mallowhc@eircom.net
Derry	Derry Genealogy Centre, 10 Craft Village, Derry, BT48 6AR, Northern Ireland. Tel: 028 7126 9792
Donegal	Donegal Ancestry, The Quay, Ramelton, County Donegal Tel: 074 9151266 Web: www.donegalancestry.com Email: info@donegalancestry.com
Down	Ulster Historical Foundation, 7 Cotton Court, Belfast, BT1 2ED, Northern Ireland Tel: 028 9033 2288 Web: www.ancestryireland.com Email: enquiry@uhf.org.uk
Dublin North	Swords Heritage Centre, Carnegie Library, North Street, Swords, County Dublin Tel: 01 8400080 Email: swordsheritage@eircom.net
Dublin South	Dun Laoghaire Heritage Society, Moran Park House, Dun Laoghaire, Dublin, County Dublin Tel: 01 2047264 Email: heritage@dlrcoco.ie
Fermanagh	Irish World Family History Services, 51 Dungannon Road, Coalisland, BT71 4HP, County Tyrone, Northern Ireland Tel: 028 8774 6065 Web: www.irish-world.com Email: info@irish-world.com

Galway East	East Galway Family History Society, Woodford Heritage Centre, Woodford, Loughrea, County Galway Tel: 090 9749309 Web: www.galwayroots.com Email: galwayroots@eircom.net
Galway West	Galway Family History Society West Ltd, St. Joseph's Community Centre, Shantalla, County Galway Tel: 091 860464 Email: galwayfshwest@eircom.net
Kerry	No current Kerry Centre
Kildare	Kildare History and Family Research Centre, Riverbank, Main Street, Newbridge, County Kildare Tel: 045 433602 Web: www.kildare.ie/genealogy Email: kildaregenealogy@iol.ie
Kilkenny	Kilkenny Archaeological Society, Rothe House, Parliament Street, Kilkenny, County Kilkenny Tel: 056 7722893 Web: www.kilkennyarchaeologicalsociety.ie Email: rothehouse@eircom.net
Laois	Irish Midlands Ancestry, Bury Quay, Tullamore, County Offaly Tel: 0506 21421 Web: www.irishmidlandsancestry.com Email: ohas@iol.ie
Leitrim	Leitrim Genealogy Centre, Ballinamore, County Leitrim Tel: 071 9644012 Email: leitrimgenealogy@eircom.net

Limerick	Limerick Ancestry, c/o Limerick County Library, 58 O'Connell Street, Limerick, County Limerick Tel: 061 496542 Web: www.limerickgenealogy.co Email: research@limerickgenealogy.com
Londonderry	Derry Genealogy Centre, 10 Craft Village, Londonderry, BT48 6AR, Northern Ireland. Tel: 028 7126 9792
Longford	Longford Genealogy, 1 Church Street, Longford, County Longford Tel: 043 41235 Email: longroot@iol.ie
Louth	Louth Library Service, Roden Place, Dundalk, County Louth Tel: 042 9353190 Email: libraryhelpdesk@louthcoco.ie
Mayo North	Mayo North Family History Centre, Enniscoe, Castlehill, Ballina, County Mayo Tel: 096 31809 Email: normayo@iol.ie
Mayo South	South Mayo Family Research, Main Street, Ballinrobe, County Mayo Tel: 094 9541214 Email: soumayo@iol.ie
Meath	Meath Heritage Centre, Town Hall, Castle Street, Trim, County Meath Tel: 046 9436633 Web: www.meathroots.com Email: meathhc@iol.ie
Monaghan	No current Monaghan Centre

Offaly	Irish Midlands Ancestry, Bury Quay, Tullamore, County Offaly Tel: 0506 21421 Web: www.irishmidlandsancestry.com Email: ohas@iol.ie
Roscommon	Roscommon Heritage & Genealogical Centre, Church Street, Strokestown, County Roscommon Tel: 071 9633380 Web: www.roscommonroots.com Email: info@roscommonroots.com
Sligo	Sligo Heritage & Genealogy Society, Aras Reddan, Temple Street, Sligo, County Sligo Tel: 071 9143728 Web: www.sligoroots.com Email: heritagesligo@tinet.ie
Tipperary North	Tipperary North Family Research Centre, The Governor's House, Kickham Street, Nenagh, County Tipperary Tel: 067 33850 Email: tipperarynorthgenealogy@eircom.net
Tipperary South	Bru Boru Heritage Centre, Rock of Cashel, Cashel, County Tipperary Tel: 062 61122 Web: www.comhaltas.com Email: bruboru@comhaltas.com
Tyrone	Irish World Family History Services, 51 Dungannon Road, Coalisland, BT71 4HP, County Tyrone, Northern Ireland Tel: 028 8774 6065 Web: www.irish-world.com Email: info@irish-world.com

Waterford	Waterford Heritage Services, St. Patrick's Church, Jenkins Lane, Waterford, County Waterford Tel: 051 876123 Web: www.waterford-heritage.ie Email: mnoc@iol.ie
Westmeath	Dun na Si Heritage Centre, Knockdomney, Moate, County Westmeath Tel: 090 6481183 Email: dunnasimoate@eircom.net
Wexford	Wexford Heritage & Genealogy Society, Yola Farmstead, Folk Park, Tagoat, Rosslare, County Wexfor Tel: 053 9132611 Email: wexgen@eircom.net
Wicklow	Wicklow Family History Centre, Wicklow's Historic Gaol, Kilmantin Hill, Wicklow, County Wicklow Tel: 0404 20126 Web: www.wicklow.ie Email: wfh@eircom.net

Websites

www.cyndislist.com

Cyndi's List of Genealogy Sites on the Internet provides over 250,000 links to genealogy sites online through a categorised and cross-referenced index. To begin Irish research, select "Ireland & Northern Ireland" from the main category index and then select from options, such as GENUKI Resources by County (select and then choose county of interest), Libraries, Maps, Records, etc.

www.ireland.com/ancestor

The Irish Ancestors website is published by the *Irish Times*. In addition to offering the ability to conduct searches for information about surnames and placenames, this site—through its "browse" facility—gives access to detailed information on record sources, including county source lists and Roman Catholic parish maps. This site also offers a free "Ancestors search" where researchers can fill in a form with details of their ancestor, the site will return a report detailing relevant sources.

www.familysearch.org.

The Family Search website is operated by the Church of Jesus Christ of Latter-Day Saints (Mormons). This site holds "the largest collection of free family history, family tree and genealogy records in the world." This site is worth visiting just for the International Genealogical Index. Select "Search" button and enter ancestor's details (name; event; year and range of years); then select Ireland as country from dropdown list and check the results.

The "Family Search Indexing" project is now under way. This is the project to digitise and index all of the LDS Church's 2.4 million rolls of microfilm and make their contents available online. It is expected to take five to fifteen years. However, public access to some of the digitised and indexed records is expected in 2007.

www.genealogical.com

The Genealogical Publishing Company of Baltimore, Maryland, has published over 2,000 genealogy books and CDs. They have now created an electronic index to 18 million names recorded in their publications. By using the "Name Search" facility on their website, which is free, family historians can search indexes to a number of Irish sources such as Griffith's Valuation, Tithe Books (for Northern Ireland), Flax Growers Lists of 1796, pre-1858 wills and 1841/1851 Census Abstracts.

www.irish-roots.net

The website of the Irish Family History Foundation. In addition to providing contact details for Ireland's network of county-based genealogy centres, this site intends to offer, on a phased basis, pay-per-view searches of the databases created by the county centres.

www.irishgenealogy.ie.

The website of Irish Genealogy Limited. A number of databases are hosted on this website, including a free, searchable index to the church registers (containing over 3 million records) computerised by genealogy centres for counties Armagh, Cavan, Derry, Fermanagh, Leitrim, Limerick, Mayo, Sligo, Tyrone and Wexford.

Bibliography

The Surnames of Ireland, Sixth Edition
Edward MacLysaght, Irish Academic Press, Dublin, 1991

This book provides a fascinating summary of the origins of over 4,000 Gaelic, Norman and Anglo-Irish surnames.

The Irish Diaspora A Primer
Donald Harman Akenson, The Institute of Irish Studies, Belfast, 1996

This book provides an overview of the story of emigration from Ireland. It will assist the family historian in understanding why their ancestor emigrated, how they left Ireland and why they chose the place where they settled.

Tracing Your Irish Ancestors, Third Edition
John Grenham, Gill & Macmillan, Dublin, 2006

In addition to comprehensive descriptions of Irish record sources, this book maps and lists all Roman Catholic parish registers and provides county-by-county source lists that are particularly detailed for census returns and census substitutes.

Researching Scots-Irish Ancestors: The Essential Genealogical Guide to Early Modern Ulster, 1600-1800
William J. Roulston, Ulster Historical Foundation, Belfast, 2005

This book, for the nine counties of Ulster, attempts to identify any surviving pre-1800 genealogical sources, such as church registers and estate records, and locations where such records can be found.

A New Genealogical Atlas of Ireland, Second Edition
Brian Mitchell, Genealogical Publishing Company, Baltimore, 2002

This book locates for every county in Ireland the following administrative divisions: baronies, civil parishes, Roman Catholic parishes, dioceses, poor law unions and probate districts; for the nine northern counties of Ulster, this work also includes the network of Presbyterian congregations.

A Guide to Irish Parish Registers
Brian Mitchell, Genealogical Publishing Company, Baltimore, 1988; reprinted 2001

This book, for every county in Ireland, attempts to locate churches of all denominations within their civil parish and provide the earliest commencement date of their registers.

Irish Libraries: Archives, Museums & Genealogical Centres
Robert K. O'Neill, Ulster Historical Foundation, Belfast, 2002

This book details, on a county basis, institutions and their record holdings of value to local and family historians.

www.ingramcontent.com/pod-product-compliance
Lightning Source LLC
Chambersburg PA
CBHW052107270326
41931CB00012B/2926